In Times
of Illness

A LION BOOK

Copyright © 1980 Brunnen Verlag Giessen, West Germany

First English language edition © 1982 Lion Publishing
based on the original German text by Kurt Heimbucher

Published by
Lion Publishing
Icknield Way, Tring, Herts, England
ISBN 0 85648 434 2
Albatross Books
PO Box 320, Sutherland, NSW 2232, Australia
ISBN 0 86760 359 3

Quotations from the Psalms are from the Good News Bible,
published Bible Societies/Collins

Photographs by Edel/Anthony, page 29; Fankhauser, pages 21, 39
and cover; Fischer/Anthony, page 5; Freytag/Anthony, page 41;
Kunkler, pages 19, 31; Horn, page 27; Lachmann, page 17; Nahler,
pages 9, 33; Penner/Anthony, page 37; Reinhold/Anthony,
page 25; Schaper/Anthony, page 45; Wich/Anthony, pages 13, 15

Printed in Germany by Ernst Kaufmann, Lahr

Author's Preface

This little book has been written to comfort and help those who are ill. Serious illness, especially long-term illness, makes us feel isolated and alone. It can be bewildering. And it certainly raises questions in our minds. It is also one of those rare occasions when we have time on our hands — time out of the busy-ness of normal life; time to listen to what God may be trying to say to us.

I was taken to hospital after an accident, and for a time I was put in a room of my own. It seemed to me then that through this enforced rest, God might — as it were — be taking me on one side to speak to me in a special way. In this book I have shared some of the things I learnt then, in the hope that they may also be of help to others.

Why?

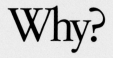

Why? Such a little word. But when we are ill it is the question every one of us asks.

Why has this happened?

Why me?

When people around are perfectly healthy, why should I be singled out?

It doesn't matter what the illness is — heart trouble, an operation involving a long stay in hospital, some illness the doctors cannot diagnose, a cancer, with all the anxiety that brings . . . The question is the same. Why?

One reason for the question may be our fear of death. We want to live. There are so many things we still want to do. We want to see our children grow up, to enjoy our grandchildren. Maybe we are less worried for ourselves than for our families. They still need us. And instead of being able to help them we are a source of worry and pain. It is thoughts like these which make us ask: 'Why do I have to go through all this? Why does it drag on so long? Will I ever be well again?

There is so much we do not understand.

Nothing seems to make sense any more. The standard answers do not begin to fit. We are like Job in the Bible, sick and bewildered, angry and bitter, hurling our questions at God.

But God understands this. He lets us question him. If Jesus himself, on the cross, cast out and rejected by the very people he had come to save, could cry 'My God, my God, why have you forsaken me?' we can ask that question too.

In our darkest moments it really seems as if God has turned his back on us. But he lets us ask the question.

And he hears us – hears our merest whisper.

Because all the time he is close beside us.

The Lord is near to those
who are discouraged,
he saves those who have lost all hope.

Psalm 34:18

The heart's unspoken pain he knows,
Thy secret sighs he hears full well,
What to none else thou dar'st disclose,
To him thou may'st with boldness tell;
He is not far away, but ever nigh,
And answereth willingly the poor man's cry.
Be thou content.

Paul Gerhardt, tr. Catherine Winkworth

Time to think

Suddenly our whole life has changed.

Yesterday we were caught up in the business of living, active, involved – part of the hustle and bustle of life. Now we have been removed from all that. We are lying in a hospital bed, or at home, totally dependent on others. For the present – and for who knows how long – life must go on without us.

Is this illness of ours just an annoying interruption? Or can it serve some purpose? I believe that in times of illness God gives us the opportunity to take stock, to take a long, hard look at ourselves. Normally there is not time. We are too busy coping with the demands of home and work. Now we have time.

The question is, are we going to take advantage of our enforced inactivity, or simply kick against it? Because it's only when we are at peace within ourselves that we can really be quiet, listen and begin to understand.

This is a time when some of the really basic questions about human life come to the surface. What, for instance is the purpose of our life?

Most of us find meaning and purpose in marriage, our family, work and hobbies, in the enjoyment of music, or sport, nature or art. Now we find ourselves asking if that is enough. Will these things see us through the crises of life?

And what about death? Doesn't the real purpose of all our lives lie with God, who made us and who offers us — now — the gift of eternal life?

What are we relying on? Our health? That hasn't proved too reliable! Or success? That's not much help either when we're lying ill in bed. We need firm ground under our feet, something that will stand up to whatever life brings our way.

And what if we die? What happens after death? That's a question we often suppress, but when we are ill it becomes insistent. And it's not enough then to say, 'Oh well, when I die it will all be over. That's the end!'

This time of illness can be a time to think. We can be open to God in a new way. At last we have some time for him. What a terrible waste if we let distractions or incessant blare of radio or TV rob us of this opportunity.

My faith securely buildeth
On Jesus, and his blood;
This, and this only, yieldeth
The true eternal good.
The life that my soul liveth,
Finds nothing on the earth;
What Christ the Saviour giveth
of all our love is worth.

Paul Gerhardt, tr. John Kelly

10

Be still, and know that I am God.

Psalm 46:10, AV

Our guide

We hear a lot today about the need to develop our full potential. We want to steer our own course with no interference from anyone. But when illness or trouble comes we realize just how little our life is really under our own control. Our independence, our self-sufficiency quickly collapses.

No one wants to be ill. Illness, like many other things in life, comes uninvited. We simply have to go through it.

So who is in charge? Who holds the cards? Does everything happen by chance? Are we alone, at the mercy of a blind fate? Or is there a hand which holds and leads us, though we cannot see it?

I believe that there is a God, that we are not left to fate or chance. And I believe that he has a plan and purpose for my life – for every life – which is essentially for our good, though we may not understand it.

God is our Father. Jesus told us that. He knew God in a way no one else can. He knew what he was talking about. If we doubt God's fatherly love and care we have only to look at Jesus on the cross – loving us so much he was ready

to die in order to save us. Jesus is our guarantee that God
loves us. Our life is in God's hands. He is in control. How
marvellous that we can place our lives in the hands of a
loving God – our Father.

The Lord is my shepherd . . .
He guides me in the right paths,
as he has promised.

Psalm 23 :1,3

Commit thou all thy griefs
And ways into his hands,
To his sure truth and tender care,
Who heaven and earth commands.
Who points the clouds their course,
Who winds and seas obey,
He shall direct thy wandering feet,
He shall prepare thy way.

Paul Gerhardt, tr. John Wesley

A lesson in patience

Being patient is not just a matter of being resigned, of putting up with the inevitable. It is something we need to practise if we are to cope with being ill.

The first thing we have to learn is to stop fretting about the appointments we cannot keep, the things we cannot do. We have to take time to be ill! We have the right to be ill!

We cannot make ourselves well. We cannot dictate to the doctor, any more than to God. And unless we learn to be patient, our anxiety may actually delay our recovery.

If we learn this lesson of patience now, it can bring us long-term gain. We *need* patience in our marriage and with our children. Impatience can really spoil relationships.

People sometimes talk about God 'being patient'. It means he never turns us away. It means that he perseveres with us. He never gives up — even when we stubbornly go our own way. He takes endless pains with us.

Patience makes us strong; helps us take a brave stand. Our illness is not God's judgement on us. Instead he comes alongside as our Father.

Knowing God's nearness, safe in his care, we can endure

whatever comes – not playing the hero, or pretending to be what we are not, but experiencing for ourselves the enabling strength of God.

You, O Lord, are a merciful
and loving God,
always patient,
always kind and faithful.

Psalm 86:15

Be not o'er-master'd by thy pain,
But cling to God, thou shalt not fall;
The floods sweep over thee in vain,
Thou yet shalt rise above them all;
For when thy trial seems too hard
to bear,
Lo! God, thy king, hath granted all
thy prayer.
Be thou content.

Paul Gerhardt, tr. John Kelly

Learning to trust

When we are ill we have to trust other people. We have to put ourselves into the hands of the doctors and nurses who look after us. We need their help. But they are people too, with personal worries of their own, and pressure on their time. So we must not expect the world to revolve around us.

Medical science has made some amazing advances. Many illnesses which once were fatal can now be completely cured. But doctors are not superhuman. They cannot work miracles. We must simply trust them to try by all possible means to get us well again. And we must also trust those who have responsibility for our day-to-day care. They may not all be equally gentle or sympathetic, but this does not reflect on their skills. The fact that we trust them is important.

God, too, is asking us to trust him in our illness. We may have given him little thought while everything was going well. Now is the time to remember him.

We may ask ourselves why the God who made the world should be concerned for insignificant people like us –

out of all the millions on earth. There is no answer to that
question. But his care and concern is a fact. The Bible tells
us so. Jesus himself assured us that the God who takes care
of the tiniest sparrow, and who clothes the wild flowers,
can be trusted to care even more for us – 'Aren't you worth
much more than the birds?'

We may not understand this. But we can trust him.
Others may let us down – as we let them down – but God
is completely trustworthy.

*Even if I go through
the deepest darkness,
I will not be afraid, Lord,
for you are with me.
Your shepherd's rod and staff
protect me.*

Psalm 23:4

In heav'nly love abiding,
No change my heart shall fear;
And safe is such confiding,
For nothing changes here:
The storm may roar without me,
My heart may low be laid;
But God is round about me,
And can I be dismayed?

Wherever he may guide me,
No want shall turn me back;
My Shepherd is beside me,
And nothing can I lack:
His wisdom ever waketh,
His sight is never dim;
He knows the way he taketh,
And I will walk with him.

Anna Waring

Talking it over

When we are very ill we have neither the strength nor the inclination to talk. We are preoccupied by pain and our own tormenting thoughts. Has the doctor really told us the truth? Is the illness much worse than he's admitting? We just want people to leave us alone. We don't know how to answer our visitors' questions. Their attempts to comfort and cheer us up, though well meant, leave us cold.

Normal conversation dries up, but we can still talk to God. Our need may drive us to prayer – or it may lead to bitterness and despair. How long is it since we really talked to God? When we pray is it simply from a sense of duty – words with no meaning? Have we ever prayed at all?

The fact is that God actually wants us to talk to him – as naturally and as spontaneously as a child talks to its father. We can tell him everything – all our doubts and fears and problems. There is no need to pretend with God; we can be completely honest.

When we pray we are not talking to thin air, we are talking to a God who listens. He has promised to hear anyone who sincerely comes to him. He will hear and will answer. We

cannot dictate how or when; we simply have to trust him.
God is our Father; we are his children. We can only see
things the way they are now. God knows all that lies
ahead, and he knows what is good for us. He may not
answer our prayers straight away, or give us exactly what
we want. But he does hear.

It doesn't matter what words we use. We don't have to
use a special language. However stumbling the words, God
rejoices to hear us call him Father.

'Great is thy faithfulness,'
O God my Father,
There is no shadow of turning with thee;
Thou changest not, thy compassions
they fail not;
As thou hast been thou for ever wilt be.
'Great is thy faithfulness!
Great is thy faithfulness!'
Morning by morning new mercies I see;
All I have needed thy hand hath provided –
'Great is thy faithfulness,' Lord unto me!

Thomas Chisholm

Trust in God at all times, my people.
Tell him all your troubles,
for he is our refuge.

Psalm 62:8

Promises

We make promises all the time.

A husband promises his wife that he will never leave her.
The young offender promises to mend his ways. When we
are ill, a friend promises to come and see us. The doctor
promises that everything will be all right.

So many promises.

Promises we sometimes cannot keep.

Promises we do not always *want* to keep.

Promises we simply forget.

So many broken promises; so much disappointment.

God makes promises too. But he stands by his promises
and keeps them all. We can lean hard on them and they
will never let us down. The Bible is full of God's promises.

'I will never leave you nor forsake you,' God says to his
people. He doesn't promise we will never be ill, or that
things will always go right for us. He says, 'I am there
beside you; I will never leave you.'

'I have called you by name,' he says. 'You are mine.' We
belong to him. He knows each one of us. There is no need
to be afraid. No one can snatch us from God's care.

'I will never forget you,' God says. Other people often forget – God never does. He is with us even in the loneliness of a hospital bed.

Charles Spurgeon, the famous preacher, collected together 365 promises of God – one for each day of the year!

Nothing can give us greater comfort or support than the promises of God. And every promise God makes he is sure to keep.

Why am I so sad?
Why am I so troubled?
I will put my hope in God,
and once again I will praise him,
my saviour and my God.

Psalm 42:11

Cast care aside, lean on thy Guide;
His boundless mercy will provide;
Lean, and the trusting soul shall prove
Christ is its life, and Christ its love.

Faint not, nor fear, his arms are near,
He changeth not, and thou art dear;
Only believe, and thou shalt see
That Christ is all in all to thee.

John Monsell

The things we take for granted

We take so much for granted in life – health, food, work, family, friends . . . It comes as a shock when one of these is taken away. But it sometimes seems as if God *has* to take something away from us before we realize that we cannot take anything in life for granted. We are on the receiving end. Everything we have comes from God – a token of his goodness.

Being ill often helps us to appreciate the little things. When I was lying helpless in hospital, these are some of the things I found myself thanking God for:

the lovely flowers in my room,

the sip of tea I enjoyed the evening after my operation,

being able to telephone my friends,

a clean and comfortable room,

people to look after me,

friends to visit me . . .

And I began to be really grateful that my accident had not been more serious. I thought of others in the hospital who were so much worse than I was. I was even glad, a few

days later, to be able to wash and shave myself and clean my own teeth!

Once we start to appreciate and thank God for the little things we begin to see everything in a new light. We become aware of all the 'pluses' – the positive – not just the things we don't have and all that is wrong with us. Things could be so much worse!

Being grateful affects our attitude to others too. Instead of taking the doctors and nurses for granted – thinking we have a right to their services, that they are simply doing a job they are paid for – we begin to realize that many of them do far more for us than they are obliged to. We appreciate being treated as human beings, people with feelings.

We are ready to give them a smile or a word of thanks. And that can help – especially when they have been on a twelve-hour shift.

Illness can teach us so much. It can change our attitudes long-term, so that when we go out of hospital we are different people. If the only thing we learn when we are ill is to be grateful, we shall be far better equipped to cope with the problems and frustrations of everyday life.

You are my God,
and I give you thanks;
I will proclaim your greatness.
Give thanks to the Lord,
because he is good,
and his love is eternal.

Psalm 118:28-29

Now thank we all our God,
With hearts and hands and voices,
Who wondrous things hath done,
In whom his world rejoices;
Who from our mother's arms
Hath blessed us on our way
With countless gifts of love,
And still is ours today.

Martin Rinkart, tr. Catherine Winkworth

Changes

Serious illness may turn our whole life upside-down. It is not easy to accept or adjust to change on this scale.

The man who has had a serious heart attack will have to rethink and reshape his whole life-style.

The person who has had a leg amputated will have to learn to walk again, to get used to the restriction of crutches or the limitations of an artificial limb.

The victim of paralysis can no longer move freely. He is dependent on others for even the most basic things. Yesterday he may have been an enthusiastic mountaineer; today he faces life from a wheelchair.

These things, and others like them, can happen so suddenly. How are we to cope? It is no comfort to be told that there are thousands of others in the same situation. Each individual has to come to terms with his own problems.

Whatever may have happened, we are still alive. God has spared our lives and he will make his purposes known to us step by step, if we ask his help.

A miner who was badly injured in a pit accident and

ended up confined to a wheelchair was able to say, 'God had to break my back in order to bring me close to himself.' That is a dramatic way of putting it. God doesn't go round injuring people. But it was true that through the loss of his limbs this man found God. In a similar way *our* loss can become gain.

It is hard to accept changes; hard to come to terms with limitations and restrictions. But we are not shut up to a life of permanent sadness. Not even illness and incapacity can stop true joy from breaking through.

Other refuge have I none,
Hangs my helpless soul on thee;
Leave, ah! leave me not alone,
Still support and comfort me:
All my trust on thee is stayed;
All my help from thee I bring;
Cover my defenceless head
With the shadow of thy wing.

Charles Wesley

I look to the mountains;
Where will my help come from?
My help will come from the Lord,
who made heaven and earth.

Psalm 121:1-2

Hope

When we are ill, we long to be well again. However long the healing process takes we always look forward to the day when we will be on our feet again and back at work. The worst moments in any illness are the times when it seems as if we are making no progress and we begin to lose hope.

The Bible, God's word, is full of hope. The whole Christian life is one of hope summed up by these words from the New Testament.

'Let us give thanks to the God and Father of our Lord Jesus Christ! Because of his great mercy he gave us new life by raising Jesus Christ from death. This fills us with a living hope, and so we look forward to possessing the rich blessings that God keeps for his people.'

Christians are not yesterday's people, always looking back. Their hope is alive. It has to do with tomorrow – and it is not limited by death. It rests on the events of that first Easter, when God raised his Son Jesus Christ from death to life. Life triumphed over death. And because he has conquered death, Jesus can say to all who follow him,

'because I live, you will live also'.

The question is, *are* we trusting him? Are we prepared to take him at his word, even when we face death? The man or woman whose hope is centred on Jesus Christ need not despair at the approach of death. It is not the end of the road. For, 'though I walk through the valley of the shadow of death, I will fear no evil: for thou art with me.' Jesus himself is with us, and he has overcome death.

The hope we have is more than vague optimism. God calls us to life – life assured and guaranteed by the resurrection of Jesus.

You will show me the path
that leads to life;
your presence fills me with joy
and brings me pleasure for ever.

Psalm 16:11

In suffering, be thy love my peace,
In weakness be thy love my power;
And when the storms of life shall cease,
Jesus, in that tremendous hour,
In death as life be thou my guide,
And save me, who for me hast died.

Paul Gerhardt, tr. Charles Wesley

The most important thing

'Health – that's the most important thing in life,' people often say. And no one would deny that good health is a very precious gift. But is it really the most important thing?

I know people who have never had a day's illness in their lives yet they are dissatisfied and unfulfilled. And I know others who have spent most of their lives under the shadow of illness, yet they possess that inner peace and joy which have eluded their fit and healthy neighbours.

So, I would say, peace is the most important thing – the kind of peace which doesn't come by our own effort and which money cannot buy; a peace which is independent of our changing moods and feelings. The peace I mean is the peace of God – peace *with* God.

God's peace is offered to us as a free gift, through Jesus' death on the cross for each one of us. His death has made peace between God, who is wholly good, and sinful human beings like ourselves. God has made peace with us and we can enjoy his peace by simply accepting the gift he offers. The peace of God within us, the protection of God surrounding us, transforms our daily life and takes the fear

43

out of death. God holds our life in his hands, and 'if God is for us, who can be against us?'

What else have I in heaven but you?
Since I have you,
what else could I want on earth?
My mind and my body may grow weak,
but God is my strength;
he is all I ever need.

Psalm 73:25-26

I've found a Friend, O such a Friend!
So kind and true and tender,
So wise a Counsellor and Guide,
So mighty a Defender:
From him, who loves me now so well,
What power my soul can sever?
Shall life, or death, or earth, or hell?
No; I am his for ever!

James Grindlay Small

Postscript

It is no accident that each short chapter in this book ends with an extract from the Psalms and the verse of a hymn.

The book of Psalms is the prayer book of the Bible. In it God's people pour out their hearts to him – their praise and thanks, but also their suffering and their deepest needs. They share with God the problems and the questions no one else can answer. Though they were written so long ago they speak directly to us, and it can be a real help to read them when we are ill.

The hymn-writers, like the men who wrote the Psalms, also have a special gift for distilling thought and speaking to our need across the centuries. Many of the hymns in this book were written by the seventeenth-century German hymn-writer, Paul Gerhardt. Because he himself went through the depths of suffering, his hymns still ring true today. They spring from his own experience, both of pain and of the lasting comfort and joy which comes from knowing God.